AF426813

A Heart as Purple as Wine

Joshua Murray-Jones

Tha Warrior-Poet A.K.A "Tha Tipsy Poet"

To Stafa,

who supported me most

through the ups,

and downs

and doubts.

To a certain fanatic

of Poetry and Vodka,

thanks for threatening

To slap me. ☺

Contents

A

Heart

As

Purple

As

wine

He saw an entire world

through hazel green eyes

and a smile.

And when that world came to its end,

he lived in the base of bottles,

sorrow, and words...

before sharing a glass

with her,

and finding home

in a brand new Earth.

Roscato

We are bound to each other

and I shall give unto you,

a boundless love.

And all across the blood orange sky,

the clouds swept with haste,

as if the world doubled time;

eager to be relieved by the moon

and her stars.

And then I saw you

and, suddenly, the world ceased;

save only the sound of your delight

at the taste of frozen yogurt.

-"I'd never forget our first date."

She wore a dress.

Maybe beige or peach

that hugged her just right

in all the right places...

Black stilettos,

complimented by her "chocolate chips"

and honey glow, hazel green eyes.

And then she twirled

and wore her smile

for his camera

"How do I look,"

she asked,

to a melted puddle

on the living room floor.

She caught the jealous eye of the sun,

envious of the way all things revolved

around her.

I was the moon,

caught in her gravitational pull.

Where he resides,

Spanish is the common language.

And when asked if he's fluent,

his response is always the same…

"My 'Spanish'

is 5'1, long hair,

eyes the color of money,

and a smile brighter than rays of the sun;

Skin covered in constellations of the stars,

beautiful to every naked eye except her own

and speaks enough Spanish

for us both."

-"Mi Amor,'
The first words you ever taught me."

She was a lion.

The dance floor was her jungle,

and her crown sat ever still,

even as she twirled.

The touch of tequila

aroused her far more

than any man ever could.

"Come have a drink with me,"

she beckoned.

And never had he ever heard

a more beautiful arrangement of words.

Like the crow of a rooster

as night becomes day;

Like the orchestra of crickets

as day becomes night,

her whispering "Papi" into his ear,

and shots of whiskey

was always the start of things.

She's an archaeologist of love;

Excavating deep into my soul,

unearthing the very essence of my

passions,

and desires.

Their story began like every story of the passionate and in love...

It was one AM. A lit candlestick, Soft tunes, and her even softer flesh; Swaddling back and forth...Slowly, modeling her lingerie, seducing him, inviting him.... Tasting and enjoying every drop of tequila that rivered down his member... Like a magnet, She pulled him in with words unsaid. His lips nickered her every curve; her every arch and every sensitive spot she possessed. With her first low whine and moan, he was obsessed. Her turn to river the tequila, he savored every drop as it fell like the Niagara unto his lips, from her most passionate spot.

She arched into him and away, he lead. That love Jones gained possession, That's the way he was bred. Green to go, oh, that Love Jones; feelings grew. The chain broken, and through her body, his feelings spew... She screamed, he gasped... eyes fluttered and toes locked... that Love jones.... In this moment, all rights were wrong, yet of no concern was shown. He pandered for air, her hands still roamed. He clenched her close, still, he had done the most...He poured more tequila and parted between her once again... And again.... And again... Until the sun rose. He, her and tequila had become the very best of friends.

"You, tequila and I. The perfect Threesome."

If I could live every night

jovial, untamed,

and drunk;

and with you,

my life would be one of

adequate perfection.

Let's get drunk. Let's take turns downing a bottle of Roscato. Only then, will I be brave enough. Let's take shots. Some of that horchata, cinnamon shit you were downing that one time... Three or four of those and maybe... just maybe, I'll be strong enough.

Let's play beer pong. The loser drinks all. The loser tells all. I would play to win.... then again, I may purposely take that "L." I'll be full of that liquid courage, and just maybe courageous enough to tell. Let's do that thing where I slurp the tequila from your navel and chase it with the lime... if we even make it to the lime. I might just slurp the tequila and decide your body is mine. I might just flip you over and trace kisses along your spine...

...and within an instant, your body would become motivation; The fine wine would redesign my imagination. You as my canvas, let me be the paint brush gliding over you.... Over and over... And over, you mouthing the melody in which I paint to; As we, intertwined, creates the world's most priceless piece of art. And to think it will have all come to fruition with just a glass of Roscato.

They say you gotta keep the night young to keep the hang over away. No doubt, I could forever get drunk on you. ❤

-"That cheap little wine we found in that

Supermarket... we owe a lot of our passion to."

When I think to

Define Poetry,

I think of all the ways

I fall to pieces,

Struggling to find

Words

Ample enough,

To describe how

Much I love

All of her

Pieces.

My lady,

my lovely…

You are my lit candle

In the darkest room,

my water source

In the hottest desert,

my crackling flame

in the coldest winter.

Teach me the

way that you ignite my soul

let us fight fire with fire,

and together we

bask each other in

wild, burn less embers.

He was a fruit kind of guy.

He could eat fruits for hours.

And his favorite fruit,

drank tequila,

and liked to dance the night away.

Her skin was soft,

like rose petals;

like velour.

Sometimes,

I would rest my head

on her exposed thighs;

the closest thing there was

to taking a nap atop a cloud.

She was a well woven cashmere…

Immensely soft

and of rare quality,

who warmed the body and soul

like a cup of winter coffee,

on a frozen night in Vancouver.

He has an appreciative love

for a good glass of white wine,

and an even more profound love

for the way that it undresses her.

He lived for the wild nights

of love and lust,

red wine;

her naked canvas

displayed over

rose petals and

silk linens;

his lustful imagination,

the paintbrush illustrating

sex had within his

poetic literature.

"I've already chosen you,"

he told her.

"In this life,

and the next,

until the sun

begins its final day,

and moon commands

its final night."

The smell of hazelnut and Irish cream would stir us both from slumber, and while we laugh and wrestle; you picking playful fights, if only to get an intimate reaction, the coffee would cool just a bit, as the last of the morning dew fled away at the sun's touch.

The kids would come down, catching us in each other's doting. And we would pull away, embarrassed, but without shame; like two high school lovers having just been discovered skipping third period to make out in the bottom stair well.

We would have breakfast. The oldest of the two would complain of his over easy eggs, and the youngest of the two would eye us curiously as we looked to one another, trading roguish smiles and expressions of adorations that the youngest would come to understand only later in life.

And as the elderly couple next door bids us a good morning, I would bid you a good day; with a kiss and with a promise of a love eternal; until the day no longer host horizons, and the night no longer host stars.

-"Imagine us."

Come,

love of my life,

love of my afterlife.

The valley is cold.

Illuminate me with your fire;

your desire.

The act will warm

us both.

She strides ever graceful

yet dangerously…

engendered fire and ice

incited from her beautiful chaos....

The eye of her own storm,

immaculate,

and law-less,

tantalizing

goddess of her own Hades.

My love,

bathe me,

bless me,

destroy me,

in your fire and ice.

What good is being a poet

in love with a woman

that words alone

could never capture

in a million cosmic years?

Pinot Noir

A flame requires consistent tinder

less it eventually fizzles out.

You need but blow a kiss in my direction.

Like a palm tree swaying in the winds;

like a dandelion dancing in a summer breeze,

I'll waiver every time.

So many miles I seem to travel

to you,

sitting, arms folded,

sunk into the opposite end of the
sofa...

"I'm fine," she says.

-"Then why so distant?"

She was never the type

to approach things in moderation.

Her love was swift,

spontaneous and immediate;

precarious and reckless;

a dicey excitement…

and always with a smile,

daring me to fall in love.

daring me to my death.

We were never meant to be

and yet,

there we were;

rebelliously in love,

lost in "potential,"

blind to the un-will of fate.

My definition of a good time… is spending untold minutes staring into her eyes. And as my eyes meet hers, we melt in each other's mind, before melting untold hours into her thighs. Her thighs.... what lies between, gives us both the greatest pleasure. But when she opens her mouth and, what spits forth from her heart, is what I consider her most valuable treasure. With that being said, I ask what is love if I'd never discovered loving her?

She clutches to a time spent before ours; from my mouth, an untruthful, unspoken session. For her, I'm just another unrighteous nigga...another learned lesson; A time ago, not thought of, yet today elevating separation.... and when she tells her girls, they'll agree I am not her greatest blessing. Soon to be the one that got away...., a lost obsession? Maybe.... Because what is love, if I'd never discovered loving her?

Everything has a flaw, yet we desire unsullied perfection. No one is invincible, yet we require unsullied protection. No one has the same mind, yet we require an unsullied connection. What one has the other doesn't and.... vice versa.... So out of a million candidates, how does one expect the only unsullied selection? And even with own imperfection, credit of my beseechment goes uncollected, and without intent to digress, the weakness that is love, charged me to press....

This, I do.... because what is love without having ever discovered loving you?

-"Compare me to the truly unrighteous,

am I so sullied?"

She wanted space.

Not the universe,

and all of the stars and moons

of it's galaxies

that I would have given her,

had I the power to make it so.

But "space."

If love

has taught me anything,

it's that I am a sucker

for short stories,

with bittersweet endings,

and bittersweet memories,

that last a bittersweet lifetime.

"I hope we can still be friends,"

she says,

still clutching his wine-colored heart.

"Sure,"

he replies,

ignoring the gaping,

bleeding hole in his chest.

- "Why can't we be both?"

He, instead

communicates with the stars

and opens his mind

to the glass of wine

the unbiased and silent rebuttal

does temporary wonders,

until eventually,

the silence ceases to be enough.

With all the power that Is embedded in me, apparently, even the mightiest of me can be mighty weak. It's become a trend; you come around, I let you in, and once again... A naked you lies next to a naked me, asleep.

When does it end? Or does it? You say it's wrong, yet you love it like I love it. Once again, your shirt is overhead, and I'm prying between your thighs; My tongue is at your neck, delivering seizures to your eyes. Afterwards, proclaiming your final goodbyes... Only to request days later if you can come by...

When does it end? Or does it? Your mind is telling you, "no," but your body can't get enough of it. Soon as you cross my threshold, my lips locking and my hands caressing boldly... Victoria shares her secrets, and all over again, your body wants to get to know me... The faucet turns on, as if inviting me to drink you slowly. And I'll savor the taste, as per you, this will be the last time, so this isn't a moment that I want to waste. Again, here I am, watching the lustful, seductive sight of you walk away.

When does it end? Or does it? Left with the proclamation that we've finally rest this case. Now days have bygone and it's on, in my home; You kissing my chest with an urgent haste. Now, lying on your stomach with my fist full of your locks, as the room resonates in high pitched swear words and out cries for God and... you looking back, throwing back, jaw dropped. Screeching that silent scream; your eyes begging with words your mouth cannot, *"Please don't stop."* Climactic conclusion, then, *"This must stop."*

- "When does it end? Or does it?"

We chase each other with endless momentum,

and then shy away once within each other's grasp…

what a strange game of tag, we play.

There was once a smile

that followed every "I love you."

Now,

just a frown with every tie,

a hiss with every sweater.

"I hate the way you dress,"

she would say.

"So that's where I went wrong,"

he thought.

"I should have focused less on love,

and more on a new wardrobe."

Tears

are often

the ink

to great

and unfortunate

poetry.

Silent,

Still,

Inaudible,

Mute,

Taciturn,

Reticent,

Soundless...

So sudden, the silence.

So sudden...

her usually voluble heart.

She was ever present…

Like sunflowers in full bloom during spring...

And suddenly slipped away,

changing with the seasons

all the same.

Leaving only her withered petals,

and broken thorns

to mark where she once blossomed.

She sent him a text; he sent her one back. Now he's speeding, going 15 over, all because a part of him is anxious to gaze into her eyes again; Low key, hoping to see love there; Low key hoping she would immediately fall into his arms and come back to him.

He sits on the opposite side, though desiring to be next to her. they talk, they catch up, they laugh, they smile... She smiles, and all over again, he's captivated. His brain screams no, but his purple heart practically tears though his chest. His eyes are peering into hers, peering into her soul, low key hoping to see love there; low key hoping she would immediately fall into his arms and come back to him.

Too attractive for her own good. Too attracted for his own good.... Dangerously poisonous; toxic even... and yet he desires only to relish in her pestilence. He admires her, unknowingly, standing there in the mystery section of the bookstore. Her chocolate chips shown pleasantly in the lighting, that seem to spotlight her perfectly. He resists the urge to hug her from behind and just hold her there, instead, choosing to move on to the poetry section. Every page he flips, and every stanza he recites, he could only relate to her. How desperately he longed to feel her love again… how desperately he hoped she would fall into his arms and come back to him.

He embraced her upon departure. They were to meet again, he hoping those were not words spoken in vain. And now, it's been a month, and in the darkness of his little apartment, he sits. High key hoping she would appear on his doorstep. High key hoping he would see love there; high key hoping she would fall into his arms and return to him. High key knowing…. that she was never coming back.

"Our last date…. Just as memorable as the first."

Some girls will

still overlook the knight,

no matter how proper the shine

of his armor.

A toast to the moon…

A drinking companion,

available always

when there are feelings

to express,

and a bottle of wine

to expire.

Love,

like war,

requires courage.

The strength to rebel

against fear,

knowing

it may scar you

in the end.

There is a burning in my chest

and the reckless self-assurance

that I could conquer Gods

given a single shot of her.

This is why I am fond of whiskies…

I think.

Shots of Whiskey

tends to mimic the same,

familiar recklessness.

And now,

You are simply just a memory,

sitting across from me

at some secluded dinner table,

wearing a smile captured perfectly

by the lighting.

I was lost in the potential of love;

you, lost in a new simple pleasure.

The happy fairy tale that

never made it to the ever after.

Even now, as I write to you

of you…

no poem makes it to the end;

purposely left unfinished;

The tiniest of hope still lingering

In a dragon slayed… a kiss shared,

And a knight escaping a tower

with a queen in his arms.

We left our love

in the clouds

waiting for us there…

floating among fiery sunsets

and written in

the constellations of

the stars.

We needed only be brave

spread our wings

look to the sky,

and glide towards the glow

of the moonlight.

Cabernet Sauvignon

Demons aren't all that bad.

I drink with mine

sometimes.

Turns out,

They don't like being "our"

demons either,

and favors red wine

All the same.

And lovers worldwide,

gave drunken kisses to

their lovers

as the new year begun

and fireworks lit the skies.

He gave a drunken kiss

to the mouth of her favorite

bottle of wine,

and fell asleep next to

where she used to be,

now, occupied by his phone.

-"New year. Same me...

Still without you."

10 Things Left Unsaid....

1.) I wanted my shirts returned. Not out of spite, but because they all now carried your scent instead of mine.

2.) I loved you most, in the moments you cuddled into me after long days of hell. It was in those moments, I felt most needed.

3.) I would always take pictures of you when you weren't looking.

4.) The best pictures I took, were of you sleeping.

5.) I still have those pictures,

6.) Sometimes, I look at them still.

7.) We don't talk or see each other anymore. Yet somehow, you still tear poems from within the deepest archives of my soul.

8.) I was always jealous of the bath scrubs, loufers… bed sheets, lotions… Anything that brought comfort to your skin that weren't my hands.

9.) I am still jealous of those things.

10.) As I am jealous, of the lips now kissing yours.

First,

we are here,

smiling, laughing

melding together

our souls.

And then

you were gone…

and my soul was left

to meld into the darkness

of the empty room.

And he jumped,

falling hard,

courageously,

vigorously,

and wit-less,

into pretty eyes,

a dainty smile,

and open arms....

And then he shattered against the sidewalk,

smearing brain matter along the pavement.

She is lost to him… And Now on the lips, on the hips, on the breast of every new lover he seeks another, or something just like that of his previous non-other. Yet none depicts the look in her eyes, the smile on her face…The way she loved or the way she purred in his embrace. So, to save face, he tries to replace, Possibly, the only real love he will have ever had.

He dates, and some make it pass the first. Maybe two. Maybe three. But that is the current record thus far. Still, the lonely nights and mental combat juggling throughout his brain; The "her" he once had, now scolding himself, " Here, now….look where we are?" And then to his surprise, colored eyes; having shown herself, to his surmise, something he thought was of love again.

Cosmic air... Dumbfounded affection... Instant infatuation; Emotional inflation. "On God! This woman is the rib!" At least... for a little while... And then... she was lost to him too. Found by another man. A previous man, by whom, she was convinced that the current man wasn't in God's plan, and what they had, they could have again.

And now... He, a new lover. On her lips; on her hips; on her breast, she possesses nothing of the previous non-other. The cycle of love in today's world is love and loss and will we love again.

-"When will the cycle end?"

And on a

summer day

In June,

I'll look to the

dandelions,

blow the seeds

and make a wish,

and pray

that the winds carry

my love to you.

99 glasses of wine on the wall,

99 glasses of wine;

1 bleeding heart,

Shattered shards at my feet,

100 glasses of wine on the wall.

He was the boat

that would have

carried her

across the seven seas.

But she chose

to be an anchor

and kept them both ashore.

Often,

I would dream of you and I,

lost in our own naiveté.

In our own world,

In a spiraling spectrum

of beliefs and doubts,

and then found

among the grapefruit

orchards of the valley,

in the embrace of each other's allure,

enamored and riveted;

whole;

until I awake

longing to return

to the orchards,

where we spiraled full circle

and the scent of grapefruit

lasted as long as our love.

If the dreams

that I have

of you

are dreams where

I don't have

you forever,

I'd rather

not have dreams

at all.

-"Whiskey to help me sleep;

The absence of dreams

To help me live."

I guess I just don't speak your love language.

Tha Tipsy Poet

is a drunk poet tonight.

And not even the drunk poet

could find her once vibrant love,

in any of the last seven beers.

Maybe 8's a charm.

Maybe it will be found

in drunken dreams.

Maybe I'll awake

in tomorrow's dawn

and cease to write of her again.

Red wine.

Red walls.

Red eyes.

Red tears.

Red wounds.

Red skies.

Red moon.

Red heart.

Bleeding heart.

Void heart.

Black tears

From a black heart,

Into black nothingness.

A black hole in a black wall.

Red knuckles.

To spend your entire life

becoming the "you"

that you are proud to be,

only to be told

that your "you"

isn't worthy….

Malicious.

Deception was an art for her.

It was almost a thing

of beauty;

the colors she spun

within every lie she told.

In my arms,

In my bed,

In every dress of hers

and sweater of mine.

In every moment of happy

and ever tear drop of sad…

In the shadow of the setting sun

and in the glow of the moonlight.

she was ever so beautiful,

always,

even in the lingering moments of

"Goodbye."

Do you think of me?

As you twirl

beneath the heat

and the flare

of those

LED lights,

the way that

I think of you,

as I twirl

in the reflection

and the bittersweet

taste

of my sorrow,

in this glass of wine?

Your side of the bed lies decadent and undisturbed, for the most part. No wrinkles, no pulled back covers; even the scent of your perfume still lingers. I can still roll over and put an arm around a you that isn't there, pull you close to me, feel your warmth against me, smell the coconut conditioning of your hair.

Your Captain America mug still sits on the nightstand. The days old coffee still there, fresh in my mind; awaiting your return to finish it off at any given moment. Your poke-dotted, pink and white socks still sit on the floor, at the foot of the bed; ever a reminder of how you won't sleep without socks, yet unconsciously remove them while floating among dreams. How I can still feel your bare feet as they rub against my own, as well as your legs, your body as a whole.

Your bra still sits on my arm chair; catching there after being removed and tossed aside while caressing and kissing you; while removing your shirt, and pulling your shorts to your ankles, and then my lips to your naked breast... down your stomach and between your legs and... well... In that sense your very aura still persists.

A bare clothes hanger still hangs amidst several others; holding button downs and sweater vest. A clothes hanger that were once home to a hoodie. My favorite hoodie... Which became yours because it was mine.

You were wearing it when you left; I watched it snatch away from my embrace; a duffle bag strap flap across its back and storm out of my apartment, slamming my front door behind it. Behind you.... shattering the nearby window in its wake... I sat on my steps for hours... hoping... Wishing... praying... my hoodie and the rose it shrouded would come waltzing back through my door. What would i even say? Don't go? Please stay? Let me love you a little longer, maybe I'll find it within you, and returned.... that last one being more a statement than question.

Your side of the bed lies decadent and, undisturbed for the most part... your Captain America mug still sits, your socks are still there, your bra still seduces me...I can still hear you, feel you, smell you... almost as if you haven't left.

-"Your side of the bed misses you."

What is a poet?

But a pile of broken

and battered emotion;

the ultimate deceivers,

in how they make decimation

look fucking glorious;

How they make bleeding hearts,

appear as flowing rivers of immortal nectar.

For but a moment,

she was everything I cared to see

and then gone;

A temporary brilliance;

A shooting star I'd wish upon.

Whiskey wets the tongue,

and his universe calls for her.

So sudden,

is she lucid among the cosmos.

Like the stars on a cloudless night;

Like the orange wheel garnish,

in the bottom of the whiskey glass.

Tell me you love me,

even though you do not.

Let the tequila form the words,

and the whiskey in me will hear them.

And we shall carry on

All throughout the night,

in love and entangled.

Drowned in alcohol,

and drenched in the sweet sweat

of tipsy, artificial love.

Until the sun rises and the hangover sets,

and the things said

as the moon commanded the night,

become ever forgotten...

"I get it,"

The young man lamented.

"I am appealing to the eye,

and maybe to the thought.

Just not to the heart."

-"Noted."

She was the permanent crease

just on the edge of my living room sofa,

next to the half empty wine glass sitting on the windowsill

where I often sat

and listened to the world cry.

The rain,

soothing as it is loathsome;

Where the cashmere finish

of the hand knitted blanket lay draped and ready;

A welcome addition to the serenity of the steam

rising from my fresh cup of coffee,

warming whole my very soul

on a frozen night like tonight.

My darling,

they say "home" is where the heart is…

I am homesick.

It is

impossible

for us,

to find again,

a love,

that was never

lost.

Merlot

"Coming"

The poet told Life.

Pen in one hand;

A glass of an old

Canadian Whiskey in the other.

"Just one more poem,

and one more hangover.

and I'll begin to live again."

He was lost and confused

Pushing alone

among his inner rainstorms.

Clothes soaked

Eyes heavy

Soul lingering on its last light,

And clutching close

The shattered pieces

of a still beating heart.

He stumbled along the guiding light,

blindly wading the storms

and found her at its end-

The girl with an umbrella

a towel

a warm fire

and glue.

Like the smell of the first page

of a new book;

like the taste of the first sip

of a new bottle of wine,

seeing her smile

and hearing her laugh

touched his senses

in ways only a new love could.

And there she sat; sunk into the plush chair situated between the mystery and poetry section of Barnes and Noble; nursing book in her hand, yet peaking just over the brim; Watching the cashier with a jealous admiration; Envious of her perfect hair and perfect make up; Her perfect smile and of the confidence in which she interacted with customers.

"If only I were so pretty... and commanded such attention," She thought, as she tore her gaze away... and unintentionally meeting his, now, burrowing into hers with an intense flare; A gaze that shouted the words that the mouth never spoke... *"You are the most beautiful girl in this room, and you have my undivided attention."*

And then he strode past the arranged coffee tables; Past the display of paper back Harry Potter collection; Past the cashier, whose eyes followed him curiously... wondering why his eyes were fixated anywhere except in her direction; Past the final shelf of the mystery section of Barnes and Noble... and sunk right into the plush seat next to the girl, blushing, with eyes wide... and curious of this strange, unusual boy.

"Here you sit, every day, envious of her... And there I sit every day, admiring you." He said. *"Watch carefully now, at the envy and admiration that we, together, will command of the entire room."*

But in that moment... the books, the cashier; The entire room all became a blur. And she saw only him, as he saw only her.

- "a mutual friend of fate,

Our meeting was pre-determined."

She was a quiet serenity

The music of swaying trees

and song birds,

along the isolated hiking trail.

There was a kind of magic

in the way that she'd looked to the stars

and found whatever clarity she sought.

How she'd look to the sky and close her eyes

as the night washed over her;

Rippling through her hair and wrapping her

in it's embosom.

How she would open her eyes and smile

and look to me as if noticing my existence

for the first time;

As if her soul had returned to its vessel

from its walk among the cosmos.

- "Take all the time

You need,

My lovely spacewalker."

Coffee for a sunrise,

Merlot for a sunset,

And you,

All the damn time.

Her skin ignited Impulsiveness.

Her perfume,

beguiling to the common sense.

Now, I smell Juicy Couture on every hoodie.

You have my undivided attention…

There are few things in life

that could possibly

matter more

than the way

your skin glows

bathed in the colors

of sunset.

From the moment I kissed you

for the first time

I knew I would always

keep kissing you,

frequently and amply;

at dinner tables,

movie theaters;

during road trips

and rainstorms;

Whenever, wherever

our lips may occupy

space together;

Never missing a chance

to experience the familiar delirium

of that first time.

"The moon is my favorite poet,"

She said.

"Unmatched,

the way it complements the stars."

She was a Spanish Wine…

Stirring nympholepsy in

every taste bud

who slurred my speech

and spun my world.

A single thought of you

does wonders to my imagination.

The image of you the fore front of my mind.

And suddenly you are laying before me

black and white; arranged beautifully

and given life

Read aloud and double tapped

In the algorithm of one's Instagram feed.

Every "like" adding validation,

and every "heart" invoking the lover

to tag or repost to his lover.

With every dedication

an unknown woman becomes you.

Ground zero. The original.

You are the poem.

-"The poem I'll never finish,

The poem I'll never get just... right."

She sometimes speaks to me in Spanish

baiting me with a smile

and an accent

if only to invoke my curiosity.

And I would fall into the trap

her, repeating the phrase

and me, mimicking the roll

of the tongue.

Laughter escaping us both;

Joy being found

in how ridiculous I sound.

The Merlot would call our lips

and we would toast and cuddle close,

lost and content

in the blissful calm

and the wishful forever

of this everlasting little moment.

She was a desert oasis;

A rare, lonely beauty

among the dry and desolate;

A quench of thirst to the dehydrated soul.

Her curves

caught my eye,

and her banter

caught my

interest.

I suddenly saw the golden glow of the sun,

reflecting its rays off the surface

of the red and grays

of the brick laid walk way.

The roses, dancing vibrantly

along the restaurant window

were suddenly pink.

The cups were purple.

The tables were blue.

Her lipstick was red.

Her sundress was a wide array

of abstract color.

And her eyes had become

 golden honey glazed brown.

She had smiled,

summoning color

to a world once black and white.

You kissed me,

and planets aligned,

and flowers sang,

and dragons roared;

and all the while,

my eyes were still closed,

my thoughts still fixed;

Lost in the cosmic command

of your lips.

I want to undress you…

Down to

your bare,

vulnerable soul.

for that,

is what I seek

to make love to.

- "Let us connect on a level

That best maximizes the pleasure."

"You don't need to give her

the world"

He told his little brother.

"Speak to her soul with your heart.

Encourage her dreams.

Hold her just because,

and take her to see the stars every so often,

and she will have all the world she needs."

In matters of love,

It has become inapposite

human nature

to fail to see

the value in someone,

until they see the value

in the someone else,

who sees them as

priceless.

The flame; once Incandescently radiant,

now, a frozen shade of its once profound blaze…

And as the butterflies fell and the dancing shadows

slowly slipped away into the void nothingness,

he extended his hand to that,

still lingering, eyeing the flame… remembering.

"Come," he said to his heart.

"There are still a many unturned pages

of a many unread chapters of a yet

to be published book,

still left to be written."

And his heart took his hand and they turned,

fading just beyond the rolling hills,

as the flame withered slowly into a small ember;

Into a cold ash; leaping into the winds,

blowing to forgotten corners of a broken earth.

Sometimes,

it's okay to

show off your

scars,

For there exist

no more

a profound proof

of your survival.

Fall in love

with a girl who

dreams...

and be astounded,

by how often she begins

to appear in yours.

Spoken truths

Becomes poetry,

When

the heart

Does

The speaking.

ZINFANDEL

She awoke

every morning

still tired

from the marathon

ran through my dreams

every night.

We bonded over ideas,

chased moments on impulse

and found love through desires.

Lust was a religion

and we, its acolytes;

Full of smiles and sin,

and whatever wine we found

ripe for the night's sermon.

He took her hand,

and all the blues

and reds and yellows

of the night's illuminations

bore witness,

and lead her into

the first tomorrow,

of the new year

with a toast

and a kiss

to compliment the

ever after

of the happy they found.

-"New year, New Love.

New sunrises to find

With her."

She is a magic kind of wine

that my tongue enjoys often;

with contents sweeter

than Moscato,

that never runs dry.

Love

is asking

to be seated in

a booth at the cafe,

but sitting on the same side

of the table.

You

are all the parts I love most,

in the moments of

freshly baked cookies

and glasses of wine,

at 2AM

on a cool, summer night.

As he brushed her hair

behind her ear

and ran his hands

gently,

from her neck,

down her chest,

and pulled her in close

from her waist;

closed his eyes

and kissed her,

all that was left

was a puddle of her

melted soul before him.

He awoke to the rays of the sun upon his face…

and also on hers, though, her sleep was never shaken. A kiss on her forehead stirred her barely conscious smile. Her wild, long, brunette hair, splayed over the pillows complimented the slight drool from the corner of her lips. Her most gorgeous lips, that he grew weak at just the thought of placing his own lips against. The entire portrait, on display before him, was the most beautiful and most priceless he had ever laid eyes upon.

Finally, the smell of coffee stirred her; the scent seemingly walking her to the source. And there he stood… waiting… marveling at his awoken prize. Hair unkempt, braless, yet making his oversized shirt her own; her intimate undies, baby smooth legs and bright smile.... He wanted to offer her the coffee, and yet he also desired to take her back to bed... She embraced him, arms around his neck as he pulled her in close, and they received morning welcomes in the form of intimacy that could only be found with each other.

They walked hand in hand along the island; her, admiring every bird and every building; every statue and palm tree… Even the sunlight and the way it cast shadows off objects in just the correct way; making mental notes and observations. She loved art. He loved her. And she never believed it, but he had always told her that there exist no piece of art, more priceless than the piece he fell asleep with every night and awoke to every morning.

The diner was crowded, though he saw no one else and heard no voices other than the angel on the other side of the table; hands covered in grease from the burger she held, and slight drop of ketchup on her nose. And then she noticed him staring and immediately she blushed. He only smiled. And as he watched her hips twist to and fro on her way to the ladies room, he could only ponder, like, *"How in the hell did I get so lucky? For I am in the most perfect place, in the most perfect time of year, with the most perfect of God's creations."* She returned, and in his palm, he took her hand, and there they sat, losing track of time… Having long finished lunch, yet staring into each other eyes, conversing about life and reminiscing of shared memories… Their love and present and future happiness.

The sun sat on the edge of the ocean; seemingly half dipped, as an Oreo cookie in a glass of milk. She sat on the sand, admiring the sunset. He sat on the sand, admiring the poem that sat next to him; until the moon relieved the sun and the stars began to admire them both. He had just enough time to remove his shirt, just before she whisked him to the shore and pounced; him, losing his balance and toppling over with her astride him.

They frenched among the shore; the waves washing over his bare chest and dog tags… The waves washing over her, now, soaked mid drift and blue Jean style shorts. She looked into his eyes and he, into hers... And both saw the rest of their lives.

-" The kids would call it a 'Bae-Cation.'"

The taste of zinfandel

becomes sweeter

when tasted from

your lips.

I am mostly inspired

by a cute

and mischievous smile;

daring me into

a dangerously, wild love;

drowned in mimosas;

with aspirations to swim naked

under waterfalls,

on some far off, secluded

Island.

A padre island sky full of Friday night fireworks.

She was admiring them.

He was admiring her.

He was a quiet man

with a quiet life;

yet every so often

desired an isolated beach

a bottle of champagne,

and her...

wearing nothing but

the sand on

her feet.

She had a spanish accent.

Her love language was

physical touch.

And so he spoke,

with his hands,

and lit candles,

scented oils,

and slow jams;

the kind our parents

made love to

in whispers...

And they conversed,

all throughout the night,

without a single word passing

their lips.

She wore nothing but her intimate things

as she danced on the patio

overlooking the padre Island waves.

Her hair swam in the moonlight

as she twirled beneath the stars.

The Zinfandel swishing and

spilling over the rim

of her wine glass.

There was magic

in her happiness; Her

smile, ethereal.

Oh, what wine does to

her soul.

Oh, the fire her

soul sets to mine.

She danced at midnight,

under aggressive gaze and beseechful drinks

in a club on 17th street.

and she was nothing to him.

She danced at midnight,

under the gaze of stars and crashing waves;

On a beach

and with a glass of Moscato,

and She was his absolute everything.

The way she bites her lip,

arches her back;

The way she would approach

in high heels,

whispering in an ear

words of a different language;

Leaving lipstick every where she kissed,

and goosebumps every where

she touched;

All forms of poetry,

to the libidinous,

lustful poet.

If love was a glass of wine,

I would drink yours

straight from the mouth

of the bottle.

She was a spanish whiskey,

aged in American oak.

I was her Black Label Chardonnay.

We would get tipsy

off the dry of zinfandel,

before getting drunk

off the sweet of each other.

Jovial and nude,

she twirled beneath the moonlight,

lucid among stars.

She enticed the poet's desires

with a poem full of curves.

A shot of rum

to dull the senses.

A glass of wine,

to pass the time.

And now his lips part,

the way her thighs do;

his tongue flutters,

the way her eyes do;

This climax marking

an end to a beginning;

"Tangerine,"

the melody that she rides to....

Down goes,

the remaining rum…

down he goes again.

It was always the little things...

The smell of

coffee in the morning,

raisin toast with

apple butter spread,

her...

In his oversized hoodie

and undies,

mixed and matched socks,

unkempt hair;

dancing in his kitchen,

smiling,

and happy.

It was always the little things.

In every dream, there she was…. Taking my hand and leading me out into some open grassy plain; where envious sunflowers seemed to reach for us and butterflies bounced ever close… as if only to get a taste of our love.

Or some old, wooden bridge… that stood over a shallow, crystal clear creek; where the trees and the plants and all of its inhabitants lined either side; where the elderly couple still kissed… At the same time, on the same day; thirty years later as they had thirty years before.

Or some cool, island shore; where waves rumbled and stars lit the sky. Where a small fire crackled in a slight dugout of the sand and Dos Equis lay waiting in a small chest, iced over; atop a silk blanket and silk pillows.

And at the end of every dream, In every grassy plain, on every old bridge, or secluded island shore;

We would embrace… and I would kiss her… and she would kiss me, and in every new place, we would fall in love, again and again.

And when I would wake, there she was, still in my embrace; curled into me in a way that said, *"I feel safe;"* Peaceful and smiling;

Still dreaming… Still running with me alongside the butterflies, on that old, grassy plain.

" There it is… I have dreamed you into existence."

A well worded sonnet,

It was;

The quiver of her body

beneath mine,

The upward thrust of her hips,

Her every kiss against my chest,

Her every breath in my ear...

I'm not a Poet...

Just a writer

With a heart,

As purple

As wine;

Often drunk

Off of its

Spilled

Contents.

<u>About the Author</u>

Joshua Murray-Jones is a 10+ years veteran in the U.S. Army, A Mixed Martial Artist, poet, storyteller, and father to a son. He was born and raised in southeast Houston Texas, where, despite being surrounded by the drug and gang life of his environment, he discovered a passion for word play and the small, beautiful things about life and the world in general. He left his home city in 2009 and has since been on the road, having lived in many places; having met many interesting and influential people. A warrior inside and outside of the cage/ring and a poet at heart. Currently, he is still looking for a place for he and his son to call home.

Acknowledgments

Mustafa Gray

Gloria Beltran

Nancy Garcia

Steven Trejo

787 Illustrations

(www.instagram.com/787illustrations)

Melissa Smith

(www.instagram.com/melissas_seasons)

Nicole Buckridan

(www.instagram.com/broken.bitches.club)

A Heart as Purple as Wine

May the wine be red,

our love, abundant,

and our world,

as alive and animated

as our poetry.

Send me your original poems/prose/quotes @

Instagram: thawarriorspoetry

Snapchat: thawarriorpoet

I will post them to my stories and tag you.

Your Poems Here...